ONCE TOO SCARED TO

SPEAK

NOW I WON'T SHUT UP

WORITAL
Dream . Work . Achieve

Dedication

To Coco: My best friend, lover, supporter, prayer partner and greatest champion. You are a man after God's own heart and I am more than blessed to be your wife. You are the manifestation of love and inspire me daily to become the best version of myself. Thank you for being the husband of my dreams and reality.

To Ambassador Emmanuel Obiako and Mrs. Jane Obiako: Thank you for raising me, believing in me, teaching me my value from childhood, encouraging me, praying for me, brainstorming ideas with me, providing me valuable feedback on this book, and loving me. It is an honor to be your daughter.

To Emy, Nkiru, Ify, and Ifeatu: My wonderful brother and sisters. The love, support, feedback, encouragement and prayers you have given me throughout our lives has made me a better human and allowed me to put forth creations like this book into the world to help others. I cannot thank you enough.

To Aunty Ngo: Woman. Thank you for making God and the truth of God attractive to me. Your love for God and your Christ-like virtues has been a blueprint for me since childhood that has helped me grow in faith and live out my God-given purpose - which includes this book.

To The Teacher Who Once Named Me 'The One Who Does Not Speak': Thank you for giving me a great story to tell and the opportunity to rise up and speak.

Contents

Introduction

*"There are three things to aim at in public
speaking: first, to get into your subject,
then to get your subject into yourself, and
lastly, to get your subject into the heart of
your audience."*
- Alexander Gregg

I was in Primary 3. A quiet and shy 7-year old Nigerian child with a moderate stutter and crippling fear of public speaking. Ironically, I had a great grasp of the English language (my test scores proved as much - thanks to living with two English scholars as parents) so my class teachers incorrectly assumed my strong writing abilities applied verbally as well and asked me to join our school's debate team.

Clueless souls.

I definitely did NOT want to and initially declined. One of my teachers was annoyingly persistent. Every time he saw me, he would remind me about the debate team and how great I'd be in it. Eventually, after enough annoying pressure, I caved and joined.

Fast forward to a few weeks later. My school had a debate competition against a neighboring school and I was selected to represent my school in the match. *My worst nightmare.* I woke up on the morning of the competition feeling sick as hell and blessed the toilet multiple times before heading off to the venue. By the time my school team and I got to the venue and I saw how large of a crowd the audience was, I was ready to run away!

How can I go up on stage in front of all these people? I look awkward. I will mumble my words. They will laugh at me!

I was paralyzed with fear. Sweating profusely, I watched as the selected team member from the other school's debate team went up on stage, made his opening speech, got a round of applause, and exited the stage. Then it was my turn. *Damn.* I heard the debate moderator call my name to proceed onto the stage. My school's debate team members patted me on the back and cheered me on with smiles on their faces. I got up from my seat and headed towards the stage, shaking while two different narratives were playing in my head...

I can do this! I am capable! I am a good communicator!

Who am I deceiving? I'm awkward, shy, and I stutter. I suck!

I climbed up onto the stage, headed over to the podium and mic at the center of the stage, took a look into the faces in the audience and....FROZE. I said nothing. I knew the words to say but I couldn't get them out of my mouth. *"Speak, Adaeze! Speak!"* Nothing. I looked over and saw our debate club teacher and team members looking at me with shock and disappointment. I saw the opposing school's debate team members looking at me and laughing. *"Speak, Adaeze! Speak!"*. Nothing. Nada. Zilch. As the tears were welling up in my eyes, I felt the mobility return to my limbs and I ran off the stage like a 100m sprint athlete.

What happened afterwards is a blur however that experience (and the hot shame I felt about it!) largely shaped my fear and terror towards public speaking for many, many years - well into my early adulthood. *Fear is real my friend.* If I'm right about you, you've either missed opportunities for public speaking engagements or run away from them due to a similar paralytic fear and you're sick and tired of it. I've been there and I'm ready to help you.

You might be wondering: *"Why should I read a book about public speaking from a woman who has just told me that she failed at public speaking when she was in the 3rd grade?"*

Good question.

While I did have an epic public speaking failure back in

Primary 3, I have had the good fortune of being plunged into many public speaking arenas between that fateful day and now, in my line of work as a Project Manager and leader of teams, stakeholder engagement liaison, and a sought-after Keynote Speaker for conferences related to project management, leadership, public health, and tech.

You might also be wondering: *"How did a quiet and shy gal crippled by the fear of public speaking become a woman that can manage projects and stakeholders, lead teams, and give keynote speeches at conferences?"*

Again, good question. *You're thinking smartly.*
The truth is that behind every successful outcome (for example, a successful speech) lies a winning 'Process'.

In this book, I will share the tried and tested 'Process' I use to **deliver great keynote speeches,** which you can use too, by breaking down the specific blueprint of a keynote speech I gave on *'The Power of Data and Partnerships'* at the 2019 Think Future Conference in Stellenbosch, South Africa to 250+ development professionals - which I received overwhelmingly positive reviews about.

Who would've thought I'd be in this position to do so?

Definitely not my Primary 3 self.

Such is life.

You and I are capable of much more than we imagine.

Join me as I deconstruct the speech delivery process and get you 7 steps closer (shameless pun) to overcoming your fear of public speaking and delivering great keynote speeches.

Let's go!

BEFORE *Speech* DAY

DEVELOP YOUR
SPEECH OUTLINE

*"Make time for planning: Wars are won in
the general's tent."*
- Stephen R. Covey

Whenever I am invited to speak at a conference, the first step I take is to develop my speech outline (well, to be fully frank, I have a mini anxiety attack first and then move into development of my speech outline. What can I say? Old habits die hard).

Warning:

We're about to get into technical, nitty gritty matters. Your first response as you're reading this step might be *"this.is.boring."*

Relax.

You know how it is. Some parts of a process can feel annoying, boring, and time consuming (e.g. the pre-implementation planning phase of a new project).

But...they are necessary.

In this case, it is *necessary* for you to understand the basic concepts of developing a speech outline and laying the foundational structure that your presentation slides, speech, and public speaking experience will be built upon.

There is no escaping it.

The good news:

Step 1 is the longest chapter in the book. Once you've

powered through the "boring", I have more exciting information for you in the following steps.

You're welcome :)

Now let's get back into it.

A speech outline serves as the foundation for your presentation - it includes the *structure, flow*, and *organization* of your speech.

The structure is generally divided into three sections:

- Introduction
- Body
- Conclusion

Introduction

This is your chance to 'hook' your audience's attention to you and your speech topic. This is where you "slap" your audience awake and get them focused on you and you alone.

Personally, I like starting off with a joke once I get up on stage that gets the audience laughing and puts them in a relaxed mood. I usually like to make a joke about the difficulty the conference host has pronouncing my first name, Nwanyibuife (it can be rather amusing to see them struggle with it) or in the case of the 2019 Think Future Conference, how wonderfully well the host pronounces it.

Fun fact:

My name means *"A woman is worth something."* I couldn't have asked for a better name however it has proven to be a tongue twister for many :)

In the case of the 2019 Think Future Conference

After kicking off with a joke, I opened my speech with a quote. *"If you want to go fast, go alone. If you want to go far, go with others."* - an African Proverb I love because it speaks to the power of collaboration as a sustainability strategy, which I strongly believe in.

Body

This is where you provide specific details about your topic, experience, and work. You share key concepts and facts, your related experience, and best practices.

Personally, I've found that sharing information in the form of storytelling and infusing vulnerability works best for me to engage audiences. I'm much more interested in a speaker who shares a story about how he or she learned the importance of strategy planning before execution of an idea or project through the process of making a wrong choice and dealing with a setback than a speaker who just says:

"It is important to conduct strategy planning before execution of an idea or project".

When I think back on the speakers I respect, whose ideas and messages lingered with me long after I listened to their speech, I find a common trend amongst them - they share a lot of stories and use personal examples! Some speakers I adore with my entire being include *Chimamanda Ngozi Adichie* (Essayist, Poet, and Novel Writer), *Michelle Obama* (Author and Lawyer), *Simon Sinek* (Author and Leadership Consultant), *Seth Godin* (Author and Business Leader), *Lisa Nicholls* (Author and Motivational Speaker), *James Altucher* (Author and Entrepreneur), and *Iyanla Vanzant* (Author and Life Coach).

In the case of the 2019 Think Future Conference

I spoke on 'The Power of Data and Partnerships' and shared stories of several data-driven healthTech projects I had managed in recent years across Africa. I shared my experience in terms of project design, stakeholder engagement, data management systems employed for the collection and dissemination of field data, and collaborative execution. I also went a step further to share the specific challenges I experienced on the projects (e.g. managing remote teams across multiple West and Central African countries, language barriers encountered, operating in security-compromised locations like northern Nigeria and DRC, operations and logistics issues, and epic stress-related burnout and health issues - I have more on this 'delightful' story coming up in Chapter 5).

Conclusion

This is where you wrap up your speech. You summarize key points of the topic you went through in more detail earlier in your speech and also provide a 'call to action' for your audience, which is the desired response you'd like them to take as a result of your speech and the information you've shared.

This is the time to make all you've been saying count.

Personally, I focus on the key takeaways and lessons that are critical to application of the topic and that resonate with me most frozen my personal experience. I like using a list system to itemize the key takeaways and lessons (e.g. a numbering or alphabet system). I also like to choose a call to action that is *specific* and can be implemented in *feasible* and *practical* ways.

In the case of the 2019 Think Future Conference I used the numbering system to highlight the top 3 takeaways from my speech (takeaway 1, 2, and 3) and I had a call to action that was specific to a perspective shift and strategy approach the audience needed to make in order to have successful project and program outcomes in their respective development fields ***(my call to action was for the audience to commit to more transparency and vulnerability with their stakeholders, which will help to build trust amongst them, and lead to stronger and more sustainable stakeholder relationships and partnerships).*** I also repeated the quote I started off with at the beginning of my speech as a way to tie it all together and remind the audience that the quote was relevant at the start of my speech and remained relevant at the end of it;

"If you want to go fast, go alone. If you want to go far, go with others."

The **flow and organization** of the speech has to do with the order your content follows, the transitions you use to indicate you're moving from one section to the next, and how you weave in and out between storytelling, facts, and lessons.

Personally, I use a straightforward method for ordering the flow of my speech content and infusing transitions:

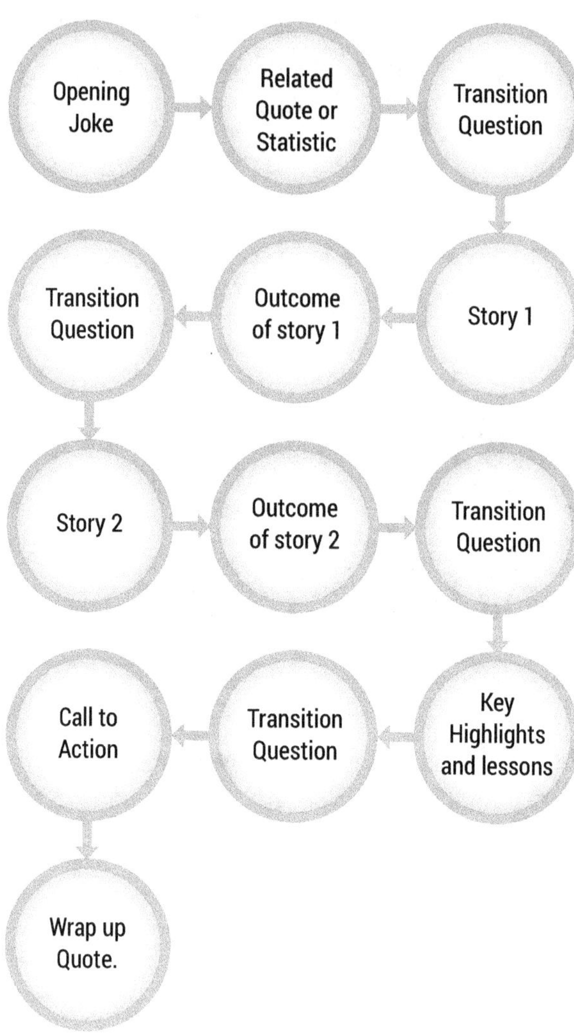

In the case of the 2019 Think Future Conference

I used the following order:

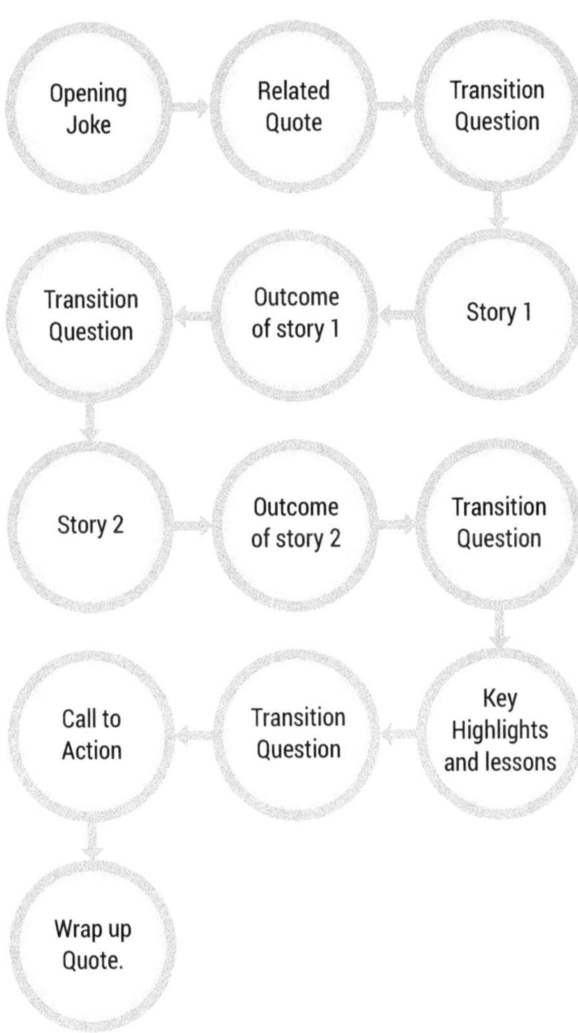

Whew! I know...the speech outline development is TIME-CONSUMING.

The good news?

Once you complete this step, you've tackled the hardest part - **getting started.** Now, the path has been cleared for you to move into the next steps of your speech preparation and execution.

Good for you!

Now let's get into some fun in Step 2 - presentation slides development.

RESEARCH GREAT PRESENTERS

*"Research: the distance between an idea
and its realisation."*
- David Sarnoff

One of the beauties of life is that we have history - records of prior experiences and people who have come before us that have done many of the things we aim to do that we can learn from. *Thank goodness. I'm always ready to take help where I can get it - past humans included.* This also applies to delivering a keynote speech. Great orators of history and great speakers of our time are plentiful; they include Martin

Luther King Jr, Nelson Mandela, Abraham Lincoln, John F. Kennedy Jr., Winston Churchill, Maya Angelou, Barack Obama, Michelle Obama, Oprah Winfrey, Steve Jobs, Chimamanda Ngozi Adichie, Simon Sinek, Brene Brown, and many more. I find videos of great speakers via Ted Talks (if you don't know what these are, remember - Google is your friend) and YouTube.

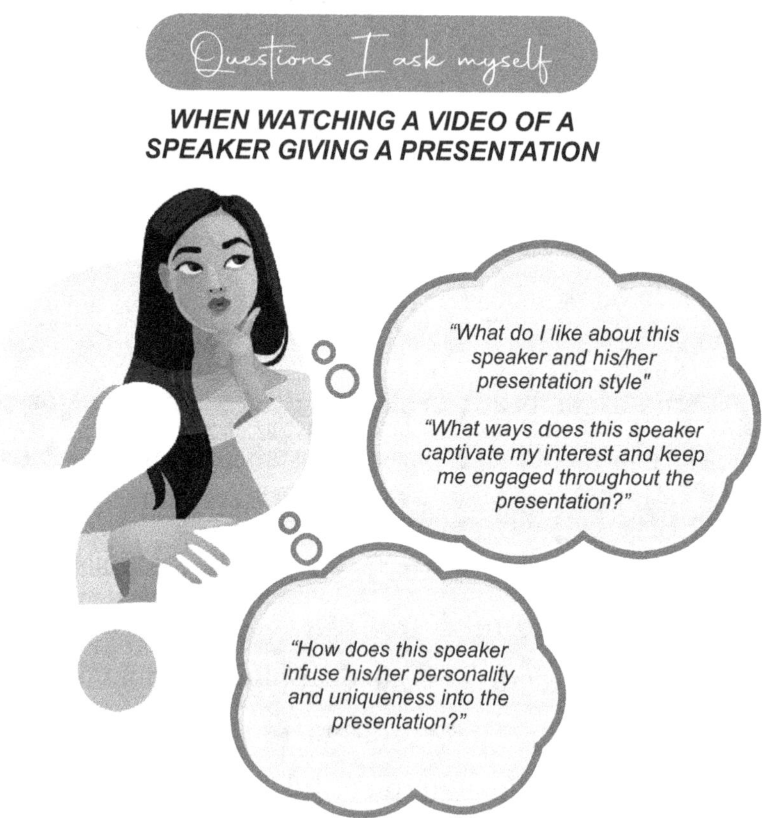

Personally, I LOVE (yes, I had to bold it) speakers that apply a storytelling approach to their presentation and weave in key lessons at different points of their story - they keep me hooked! I also like when speakers have a unique, signature look that sets them apart (e.g. a funky hairstyle), as well as when they infuse parts of their personality (e.g. cultural colloquialisms, jokes, and more). One of my favorite speakers is Chimamanda Ngozi Adichie. Aside from her strong command of both the English and Igbo languages and her eloquent speech abilities, I appreciate how frequently she uses stories throughout her speeches to illustrate her points and her proud Afrocentric look (typically a big afro and African ankara print dresses. Could she be any more mesmerizing?). I should mention that she's an Igbo Nigerian woman from Anambra state with a long ass name - just like me :)

In the case of the 2019 Think Future Conference

My research included watching multiple Ted Talk videos from speakers including Chimamanda, Simon Sinek, and Brene Brown. All of their speeches inspired me in different ways (from speech flow and pattern to owning a signature look to infusing personality / vulnerability). They're simply brilliant speakers and I learned a good bit about public speaking from these three.

Once you've done this research and have a good sense of what you like versus what you don't like in presentations, and determine how you want to introduce your own personality into your speech (very important - you should still plan to be YOU during your speech), it's now time time to get into some more deliciousness...DEVELOP PRESENTATION SLIDES.

DEVELOP PRESENTATION SLIDES

"Your Slides should be a billboard, not a document!"
- Lee Jackson

Presentation slides time! This is when I begin to have real fun with the process...I like clean, pretty, and organized presentation slides. They make me happy. What can I say? It's my inner nerd's territory.

Typically, the organizing body of a conference or summit has set guidelines for keynote speeches and presentations. This helps to guide your development of your presentation.

Personally, I like to confirm the presentation guidelines from the organizing body and then move into development.

I don't want any confusion. Spell it out for me...before we end up with "stories that touch" :)

In the case of the 2019 Think Future conference

The speech/presentation guidelines were as follows:

- 15-20 minutes
- 'Less text, more imagery' per slide
- TED Talk Style
- Save and submit as a PowerPoint file

This was very helpful information and made the slide presentation development process much smoother than it would have been if there were no guidelines to work with. Knowing the speech duration and preferred presentation format (and researching Ted Talks - watching several on YouTube and using Google to find samples of Ted Talk slides) helped inform the following decisions I made:

1. A max of 15 slides

Based on prior presentation experience, I estimated I'd spend an average of 1 minute per slide, for a total of 15mins.

Note: I included an additional time buffer of 5 minutes for i. my introductory joke when I first get on stage ii. a key point I might need to expand upon that will keep me a little over 1 minute on one or two of the slides.

2. Keep Text Stupid Simple

I limited the text per slide to one liners or a bulleted list of 3-5 points or a question or a quote. It can be so annoying when slides are overcrowded with text...scary even.

3. Make Imagery the MVP

There's always the star a.k.a. Most Valuable Player in a team. For my presentation, it was imagery. Related graphics and/or pictures were included on each slide, and an audio/video clip was also added where applicable.

Fun Fact: The development of my presentation slides for the 2019 ThinkFuture conference was a collaborative effort between my husband (a creative media professional) and I. I handled the written content and story flow, and he handled the slide design layout and graphics to go with each slide. The slide presentation was beautiful and a major highlight of my presentation that got really positive reviews. Thank you hubby of life! You're the real MVP

In the event that you're working on your slides alone, don't be discouraged - I've also done so on several occasions! You can pull inspiration from presentations others you know have done, Google searching 'examples of great slide presentations', and using related photos / videos you have saved in your personal folders or getting stock images from Google.

You got this...no shaking :)

Now let's move into the next right step - PRACTICE.

Gehn gehn.

DON'T INSULT YOURSELF ....PRACTICE

"If you don't practice, you don't deserve to win."
- Andre Agassi

"There is no glory in practice, but without practice
there is no glory."
- Vladimir Horowitz.

I'm laughing as I write this chapter. I'm laughing because while I know the importance of consistent practice when it comes to being great at anything and preach it religiously, I have been guilty at times of letting my ego reign supreme and allowing myself to think that "I don't need that much" practice in areas I have established a decent grounding in - e.g. writing, communicating a major idea or strategy to my project team, developing a project budget, and....giving a speech.

I remember a stakeholders forum I was asked to deliver a presentation at several years ago. The room was going to be made up of about 15 stakeholders from government, funding agencies, and local implementing partner organizations. I was the manager of a health systems strengthening project and had a team of about 100 people working with me. We had been working on the project for some time and I was meant to deliver a 10 minute progress update presentation to everyone.

I barely practiced in advance. I kept pushing it off.

"Why do I need to practice much anyways? Is it not the project I have been managing for some time now? I know the updates I need to share. I'm good!"

Ego oh!!! What a terrible thing.

When presentation day came, I did NOT deliver greatly. To my surprise, I was anxious at the start when I saw all the eyes looking my way, had a brain fart mid-way through and forgot a major point I was trying to make, went past my 10 minutes time slot, and used a good ol' number of *umm's* during my speech that made me sound rather nervous and unprepared - *which I was.* That was a great teaching moment for me on the danger of ego and the importance of humility (I ate the entire humble pie that day!) and it gave me a new appreciation of the importance of practice and preparation.

The more you practice your speech and presentation, the more confident you become with the content, how you're delivering it, and ensure you deliver it within the time stipulation provided.

Do not be deceived...poor practice leads to poor outcomes.

DURING PRACTICE

Personally, since that shameful experience, I ensure to carve out ample time (at least 1-2weeks in advance) to practice several run throughs of any presentation or speech I have to give - whether it is for 5mins, 20mins, or an hour. It makes a difference!

In the case of the 2019 Think Future Conference

Once my speech outline and presentation slides were developed (about 3 weeks in advance of the conference), I began practicing my presentation, from start to finish - how I'd open my speech and the quote I'd lead with, the transition questions I'd use, the stories I'd tell, how I'd close the speech, how I'd walk around the stage and for how long, when I'd look from the left side of the crowd to the right, and more. I practiced at work in the conference room, at home in my living room, and even the day before my speech in the hotel room I was lodged in. I practiced, practiced, practiced...until I earned full confidence in what I was saying and how I was saying it.

Practice my friend...don't let the shame that caught me that fateful day catch you too.

After you've practiced to the point of earned confidence, now you move to the battlefield step...TAMING YOUR BEAST WITHIN.

ONCE TOO SCARED TO SPEAK NOW I WON'T SHUT UP

Speech
DAY

TAME YOUR
BEAST WITHIN

*"It's not what you are that holds you back,
it's what you think you're not."*
- Denis Waitley

We all have a beast within. The beast has one primary assignment - to ensure we do not become the best version of ourselves.

The beast uses several means to achieve this goal - doubt, ego, insecurity, pride, and self-sabotaging thoughts replayed in our minds like *"I'm not good enough to do this!"*, *"I'm too stupid to do that!"*, *"I'm too young and unqualified to try!"*, *"I'm too old to switch careers, my time has passed!"*, *"I can't be a good speaker because I have anxiety and I stutter!"*

You might think I'm being too dramatic.

A beast? Calm down girl, it ain't that deep.

Oh, but it is.

If it makes you feel better, you can refer to the beast by a more commonly used name like *Imposter Syndrome*, that's fine - as long as you acknowledge its existence.

Why?

Because it is only what we acknowledge that we can address and manage.

I want you to be able to combat feelings of severe inadequacy and self-doubt when they creep up; one of the best opportunities for such feelings to arise is on the day of your scheduled speech and presentation.

It's possible that you can go through the process of developing your speech outline and presentation slides, researching and studying great speakers, practicing upto to a great point of confidence, and still find yourself on the day of your speech with either mild, moderate, or strong feelings of inadequacy and doubt creeping in.

What do you now do?

Again, I'm here to help.

My beast within and I have a very amusing relationship. Some days, I battle it and win; other days, it comes doubly prepared to tussle and knocks me off my feet - *the little bugger*. That being said, I've become quite experienced at winning the battle over the beast when it comes to public speaking and giving keynote speeches - the one thing that once terrified me most in life.

There are several ways to prepare for battle against the beast a.k.a Imposter Syndrome and win including meditating, praying, reciting positive affirmations, visualizing yourself on stage having a great experience with the audience, listening to uplifting music, wearing an outfit that makes you feel comfortable and powerful, and getting encouragement from your loved ones.

Personally, I like employing a mix of several of the earlier mentioned tactics to really build my mental state up and provide a great 'punch in the gut' to the beast.

In the case of the 2019 Think Future Conference

- I started my morning with Our Lord's Prayer and asked the Holy Spirit to give me the sound mind, clear words, and good cheer to have a great speech.

- My husband and I prayed for a successful outcome that morning and he told me he believed I'd do well (thank you hubby!)

- My father reminded me beforehand that I can do anything I set my mind to and he also believed I'd do well, which I remembered that morning (thank you Daddy-o!)

- I danced to the song 'Victory' by Eben on repeat in my hotel room while getting ready that morning. It lifted my spirit greatly and I felt on top of the world (thank you Eben!).

- I wore a vibrant African ankara pant suit with black flats (FYI - I'm not a fan of heels and do everything I can to avoid wearing them. They hurt my size 12 feet - I can't kee myself). The outfit made me feel like an African queen ready for battle. Yes, I have a flair for the dramatic :)

"While clothes may not make the woman, they certainly have a strong effect on her self-confidence, which, I believe, does make the woman."
- Mary Kay Ashe

Fun Fact: my brilliant sisters Nkiru and Ify played a key role in my stage look at the 2019 Think Future Conference. I planned to wear an ankara print dress — Ify did not agree. She sent me a picture of an ankara pant suit and said "This is what you should wear". I obliged. Nkiru picked the specific print pattern and color. The outfit was a hit and matched the 'lioness' hair I had chosen. Thank you my sisters of life! :)

Photo courtesy of the 2019 Think Future No.2 conference

By the time I left the hotel room, I was super confident and excited. I was ready to get on the stage and give a proverbial finger to the beast.

And that is how you should feel on the day of your speech - ready to shine and win the battle over your beast.

Now, let's move into what all this is leading you upto...your time to shine and TELL US WHAT YOU KNOW.

Step 6

TELL US WHAT YOU KNOW

*"Storytelling is the most powerful way to put ideas
into the world today."*
- Robert McKee (Theologian)

*"Facts don't persuade, feelings do. And stories are the
best way to get at those feelings."*
- Tom Asacker

Photo courtesy of the 2019 Think Future No.2 conference

Photo courtesy of the 2019 Think Future No.2 conference

The time has finally come, yay!

You've prepared, practiced, tamed your beast within, and now you stand on stage before your audience. All your effort, work, and prayers have led you here.

Now what?

Tell us what you know.

That is what your audience has waited for. That is what your audience woke up in anticipation to hear and learn from. We're ready.

Tell us your stories. Tell us your experiences. Tell us the relevant concepts and statistics about your topic. Tell us your lessons learned and best practices gained. Tell us your jokes, if you're inclined to. Share some of your vulnerabilities. Connect with us. Engage us.

Make us remember your name.

Good questions.

Maya Angelou said *"I've learned that people will forget what you said, people will forget what you did, but people will never forget how you made them feel."*

Personally, I remain mindful of this quote on speech day (I love Maya) and intentionally walk onto the stage ready to make the audience feel connected to me and the message I'm sharing.

In the case of the 2019 Think Future Conference

- I started with a **joke** about how conference hosts typically mispronounce my first name and my gratitude that the Think Future host got it right - kudos to her :)

- I shared an **African proverb** on the importance of partnerships for success and sustainability *("If you want to go fast, go alone. If you want to go far, go with others.")* Also a beloved saying of mine.

- I shared the **story** of my earlier project management days when I used to pride myself on being *"a strong woman that can do bad all by myself"* and how that led to anxiety, burnout, stress, and terrible health issues that manifested physically (extreme weight loss and fatigue, multiple breakouts and dark marks on my skin, and excessive dry skin; I looked dreadful). That was a great teaching moment on the importance of collaboration, humility, and self-care. Now, I'm a self-care princess!

- I shared **stories** of successful data-driven health systems strengthening projects I had worked on that were a result of collaborative project design, planning, and execution. A favorite quote of mine I referenced: *"At the heart of any data-driven project or program that achieves high impact and scale is partnership. It is a minimum requirement." - **Nwanyibuife Adaeze Ugwoeje***

- I shared **lessons learned** from successful and failed projects I've managed

  - Key stakeholders from private and public sector need to be part of strategic program planning (from government officials to funding partners to implementing organizations to community members)
  - Successful partnerships are built on common interest and trust; trust is dependent on transparency and willingness to share experiences

(successes AND failures), lessons learned, and best practices
- Strong data management systems are inclusive of innovative storage methods (encrypted geodatabases) and active feedback loops (real-time visualization dashboards, WhatsApp groups)
- Documentation and knowledge management is critical for historical record keeping, training, and efficient decision-making purposes.

- I closed out with a **call to action** (my call to action was for the audience to commit to more transparency and vulnerability with their stakeholders, which will help to build trust amongst them, and lead to stronger and more sustainable stakeholder relationships and partnerships) and repetition of the African proverb I started my speech off with (*"If you want to go fast, go alone. If you want to go far, go with others."*)

Afterwards, several conference participants came up to me to applaud my speech and the positive impact it had on them. One woman said:

"You were amazing up there. I wish I could do what you did. You're a phenomenal woman."

Yes, I gave a great speech. Yes, I was prepared and knowledgeable about what I spoke on (management and execution of data driven projects, leadership of teams, and effective stakeholder engagement). No, I didn't just wake up on D-day and deliver a great speech.

Behind every successful outcome (for example, a successful speech) lies a winning 'Process'.

I followed a process, prepared, practiced, and told the audience what I knew.

In a bid to ensure YOU have successful speech outcomes too (in your professional and personal life), I've shared my process for delivering great keynote speeches in this book - I hope you use it and customize it when necessary (depending on your audience).

Now let's move to the final and critical part of the keynote speech experience...CONDUCT A POST-MORTEM REVIEW.

AFTER
Speech
DAY

CONDUCT A POST-MORTEM REVIEW

"Self reflection is the school of wisdom."
- Baltasar Gracian

Post-mortem reviews are usually done at the end of projects to assess what went well, what didn't, and what could be done differently in future. We can consider delivering a keynote speech as a 'project' - it involves planning, implementing, and closing, which are all project phases.

Nwanyibuife, why do I have to do a review? It's done. I have finished my speech - I don't get a do over!

Yes, you're done with THIS speech. But...do you intend for it to be your last one?

If the answer is no and you'd like the opportunity to deliver more speeches, share the knowledge you know with others, and do even better next time, then you better do a post-mortem review.

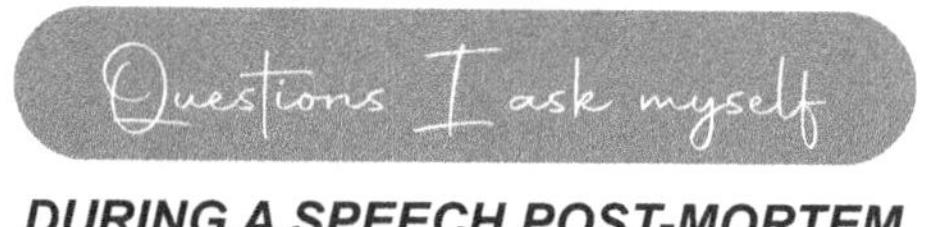

DURING A SPEECH POST-MORTEM

Personally, as a Project Manager and public speaker, I love doing post-mortem reviews - *geeky, I know*. I find it to be such a useful self-reflection exercise and I always come out of it with a stronger sense of what works well in my speeches that I should keep doing and what doesn't work well that I should kick to the curb.

In the case of the 2019 Think Future conference

I did my post-mortem the day after delivering my speech, when I had some downtime. Some of the points I reviewed include:

What Went Well

- I got the audience laughing and relaxed from the beginning with a joke
- I got the audience to connect with me as a person and the points I made through vulnerably sharing stories of personal project successes and failures
- I transitioned from one section to another with questions to the audience that kept them engaged
- I summarized key lessons and best practices towards the end of the speech
- I ended the speech with a clear and practical call to action for the audience

What Can I Do Better Next Time

- I spoke too fast at certain points (I can speed talk for the gods!); next time, I can afford to slow down more.
- I could have included more images in the slides of myself and the project teams I told stories about in different settings (project planning phase, implementation phase, and closure). I had a couple photos in there however additional ones could have been included to tell a more holistic visual story.

Every time I do a post-mortem for one speech, my next speech ends up better because I apply the key lessons from the exercise.

Don't discount post-mortems.

"The more reflective you are, the more effective you are."
- Hall and Simeral

C'est la vie :)

Conclusion

Since we've made it to the end of the book, it only seems right to round us up with a line from one of my favorite Boyz II Men songs - End of The Road.

I had one main goal with this book - to help you start delivering great keynote speeches by telling you the truth about what it takes to do so (7 steps) from my personal experience.

I hope the goal was achieved.

I hope you consider yourself more equipped now than ever before to get up on a stage (or in front of an audience of any kind - at work, at home, at social events, on social media, etc) and *tell us what you know* in a way that makes us feel connected to you and your message.

I hope you now know to call your beast by its name (e.g. Imposter Syndrome) and battle it squarely In the eye with preparation, practice, prayer, positive affirmations, and early morning jam sessions in your arsenal.

I hope you now know that social anxiety can make you feel nervous to speak in public but it cannot stop you from making an effort, putting in work, and delivering a great speech.

I hope you know that if I (a quiet and shy Nigerian gal that failed at public speaking in Primary 3 who sometimes still stutters and deals with bouts of social anxiety in adulthood) can deliver great keynote speeches at conferences to audiences of 250+ renowned professionals, then YOU definitely can too.

And lastly, I wish you what I wish myself...that you go forth in faith and love to master the art of great speech delivery (with YOUR unique flavour included), connect with others through vulnerable storytelling, and use public speaking as one of the ways you make a positive impact in your community, society, and world at large.

As you do so, I'd love for you to share your experiences with me - send me an email or chat me up on social media. I mean it. You can find me via **'Nwanyibuife Ugwoeje'** on LinkedIn, Twitter, Facebook, Instagram and more.

Take care and God bless you.

Signed,
Once Too Scared To Speak, Now I Won't Shut Up